Matt.

FEBRUARY MONTHLY ACTIVITIES

Written by Janet Hale
Illustrated by Blanqui Apodaca and Paula Spence

Teacher Created Materials, Inc.
P. O. Box 1214
Huntington Beach, CA 92647
© *Teacher Created Materials, Inc. 1989*
Made in U. S. A.
ISBN 1-55734-156-7

TABLE OF CONTENTS

Table of Contents
(cont.)

Introduction

February Monthly Activities provides 80 dynamic pages of ready-to-use resources, ideas and activities that students love! All are centered around the themes, special dates and holidays of the month.

A complete "month-in-a-book," it includes:

- *A Calendar of Events* - ready to teach from and filled with fascinating information about monthly events, PLUS lots of fun ways you can apply these useful facts in your classroom.

- *A Whole Language Integrated Teaching Unit* - theme-based planning strategies, projects, lessons, activities, and more that provide a practical, yet imaginative approach to a favorite seasonal topic.

- *People, Places and Events* - an exciting series of activities that relate to the daily events in the Calendar of Events, and provide an innovative way for students to reinforce skills.

- *Management Pages* - a supply of reproducible pages that take you through the month, providing a wealth of valuable organizational aids that are right at your fingertips.

- *A Bulletin Board* - featuring a "hands-on" approach to learning; complete with full-size patterns, step-by-step directions, and tips for additional ways you can use the board.

Ideas and activities are also included for:

math	*geography*	*literature ideas*
art projects	*social studies*	*cooking*
reading	*stationery*	*reports*
science	*creative writing*	*seasonal words*

February Monthly Activities is the most complete seasonal book you'll ever find, and its convenient, reproducible pages will turn each month into a special teaching—and learning—experience!

Using The Pages

February Monthly Activities brings you a wealth of easy-to-use, fun-filled activities and ideas that will help you make the most of February's special themes and events. Although most of the activities are designed to be used within this month, if the holidays and traditions vary in your location, you may easily adapt the pages to fit your needs. Here are some tips for getting the most from your pages:

CALENDAR OF EVENTS

Each day makes note of a different holiday, tells about a famous person or presents a historical event. A question relating to each topic is provided (answers are on page 76). Teachers can use these facts in any number of ways including:

- *Post a copy of the calendar on a special bulletin board. Each, day assign a different student to find the answer to that day's question. Set aside some time during the day to discuss the question with the whole class.*

- *Write the daily fact on the chalkboard. Have students keep a handwriting journal and copy the fact first thing each morning. They must use their best handwriting, of course!*

- *Use a daily event, holiday or famous person as a springboard for a Whole Language theme. Brainstorm with the class to find out what they already know about the topic. Explore the topic through literature, the arts, language and music.*

- *Older students can write a report on any of the daily topics. Younger students can be directed to draw a picture of the historical event or figure.*

- *Have students make up their own questions to go along with the day's event!*

- *Assign each student a different day of the calendar. Have them present a short oral report to the class on that day's topic.*

- *Use the daily events for math reinforcement. Ask how many: Days, weeks, months and years since the event occurred (for a real brain teaser, have students compute hours, minutes and seconds).*

- *Use in conjunction with the People, Places and Events section (pages 32 - 46).*

BLANK CALENDAR

Copy a calendar for each student. Have students use them to:

- *Write in daily assignments; check off each one as completed.*

- *Set daily goals—behavioral or academic.*

- *Copy homework assignments.*

- *Fill in with special dates, holidays, classroom or school events.*

- *Keep track of classroom chores.*

- *Use as a daily journal of feelings.*

- *Make ongoing lists of words to learn to spell.*

- *Answer the Question of the Day (see Calendar of Events).*

- *Record daily awards (stamps, stickers, etc.) for behavior or academic achievement.*

- *At the end of the day, evaluate their attitude, behavior, class work, etc. and give them a grade and explanation for the grade.*

- *Log reading time and number of pages read for free reading time.*

- *If there are learning centers in the classroom, let students keep track of work they have completed at each one or copy a schedule of times and days they may use the centers.*

- *Each day, write at least one new thing they learned.*

MANAGEMENT PAGES

Nifty ideas for extending the use of these pages.

- **Contracts** — *Help students set long or short term goals such as keeping a clean desk, reading extra books or improving behavior.*

- **Awards** — *Show students you appreciate them by giving awards for good attitude, helping, being considerate or for scholastic achievement. Students can give them to each other, their teacher or the principal!*

- **Invitations** — *Invite parents, grandparents, friends or another class to a classroom, school or sports event.*

- **Field Trip** — *Use for class trips or have students use in planning their own field trip to another country or planet.*

- **Supplies** — *Tell parents when you need art, craft, classroom, physical education or any other kind of supplies.*

- **Record Form** — *Place names in alphabetical order to keep track of classroom chores, completed assignments, contracts or permission slips.*

- **Stationery** — *Use as a creative writing pattern, for correspondence with parents, or for homework assignments.*

- **News** — *Fill in with upcoming weekly events and send home on Monday or let students fill in each day and take home on Friday. Younger students may draw a picture of something special they did or learned.*

- **Clip Art** — *Decorate worksheets, make your own stationery or answer pages. Enlarge and use for bulletin boards.*

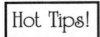

Be sure to look for the hot tips at the beginning of each section—they provide quick, easy and fun ways of extending the activities!

February Highlights

- Calendar of Events
- Spelling Activities
- Story Starters
- Gameboard
- Poetry
- Art Project
- And More!

Hot Tips!

Use clip art (p. 63) for name tags when going on a field trip, or when guest speakers come to your class.

Allow students to design the "background" of your calendar dates by voting. Then, give each child a 3" x 4" piece of paper to draw the picture (for example, Abraham Lincoln's stove pipe hat). Finally, use a black felt marker to write dates and put up onto blank calendar background (p. 10 - enlarged).

FEBRUARY

February is known as the "love" month. It is the second month of the year. It is also the shortest month. February used to have 30 days until Julius Caesar "stole" a day and put it in July!

Flower: Violet

Birthstone: Amethyst

44 days until Spring! **5** *What is your favorite season?*	**Queen Elizabeth II was crowned in 1952.** **6** *Where was her coronation ceremony held?*	**Charles Dickens' birthday** **7** *What is an author?*	**The Boy Scouts of America was established in 1910** **8** *What is the Boy Scout motto?*
	**First public school established in 1635** **13** *In which city was this school?*	**Valentine's Day** **14** *Who is Cupid?*	
International Friendship Day **19** *Who is your best friend?*	**Student Volunteer Day** **20** *What does "volunteer" mean?*	**Lucy B. Hobbs, the first woman dentist was born** **21** *How many teeth does an adult have?*	**George Washington was born in 1732.** **22** *When was he elected 1st president of the United States?*
Chateaudon International Dog-Derby **25** *What is a dog sled?*	**Buffalo Bill born in 1846** **26** *What was his real name?*		**Grand Canyon National Park established - 1919** **27** *How wide is the widest part of the canyon?*

Freedom Day **1** *What is freedom?*	**Ground Hog Day** **2** *Did he see his shadow?*	**Elizabeth Blackwell, 1st woman doctor, was born in 1821** **3** *What is a physician?*	**Charles Lindbergh's birthday -1902** **4** *When was his famous cross-Atlantic flight?*
Swiss Snow Sculpture Day **9** *What countries border Switzerland?*	**The 41st day in the year.** **10** *How many days until New Year's?*	**National Inventor's Day** **11** *What would you like to invent?*	**Abraham Lincoln born in 1809** **12** *Where was he born?*
Canada's Maple Leaf flag adopted **15** *Do you know in what year?*	**Edgar Bergen born in 1903** **16** *What is a ventriloquist?*	**Bald Eagle Day** **17** *What does "endangered species" mean?*	**The planet Pluto was discovered in 1930** **18** *How many planets are there in our solar system?*
	First bathtub installed in the White House - 1851 **23** *How long ago was that?*	**Estonia Independence Day** **24** *Where is Estonia?*	YOU ARE HERE!
59th day of the year **28** *How many days until Christmas?*		**Leap Year Day** **29** *When does Leap Year occur?*	**Other holidays:** ■ *Black History Month* ■ *Dental Health Month* ■ *National Patriotism Week (3rd week in Feb).* ■ *Chinese Lunar New Year (first new moon between January 21 and February 19).*

SUNDAY	MONDAY	TUESDAY	WEDNESDAY	THURSDAY	FRIDAY	SATURDAY

February Words and Activities

February Word Bank

freedom	cupid	shadow	cloudy
slavery	letter	ground hog	stamp
Lincoln	card	scared	stars
president	heart	happy	party
first	brave	soil	year
last	hero	sunshine	leap
love	honest	dirt	hibernate
lace	winter	Washington	hole

Spelling Activites

Use the Word Bank above to complete one or all of the activities suggested. Students may work independently or in teams.

- *Use the clip art to cut out heart, presidents, ground hog shapes (p. 63). Have students classify spelling words and write on corresponding shape.*

- *Make a Valentine card. Place all of the "ar" words on one side. Write 3 - 4 "ar" sentences on the opposite side.*

- *Make a homonym and synonym chart. Have students place pairs of words on the appropriate side.*

- *Use cinnamon red hot candies to spell out the words at an activitiy center.*

- *Set a mirror up in the room with a list of the spelling words next to it. Allow students to come over, during free time, hold up mirror and say the words while looking in the mirror. Then have students finger spell the words on the mirror.*

Story Starters

☐ February is an exciting month for writing! Two famous U.S. Presidents were born during this month, and it contains lots of holidays and special events...such as the Chinese Lunar New Year, Boy Scout's birthday, Valentine's Day, National Inventor's Day, and many, many more!

☐ Decorate your bulletin board with Big Patterns from pages 65-67 and give it the title "February Fun."

☐ Provide a pocket with these story titles on strips. Students can use these during their free time or during creative writing time.

My Freedom

My Friend, Mr. Lincoln

Mr. Ground Hog and His Giant Shadow

The Missing Chinese Kite

My Invention

Cupid's Broken Arrow

My Best Friends

A Trip to Pluto

The Heart Monster

I Am George Washington's Brother/Sister

The Year February Didn't Leap

I Knew Buffalo Bill

☐ Discuss what a biography is. Read a simple biography about Abraham Lincoln or George Washington. Then list, in outline form, the parts of a biographical story. Assign students to write a biography of a person they like or admire.

☐ A play is simply a story that has been divided up into parts. These "roles" are what each person says. Divide the class into teams and have them write a one-act play. To complete the project, have each team make scenery and present their plays to the class...why not invite parents, or even another class!

Name _____ Date _____

Ground Hog Open Worksheet

Directions: _____

1.

2.

3.

4.

5.

6.

Valentine's Day Clues

All the answers to the following clues can be found in the word Valentine. The first one has been done for you.

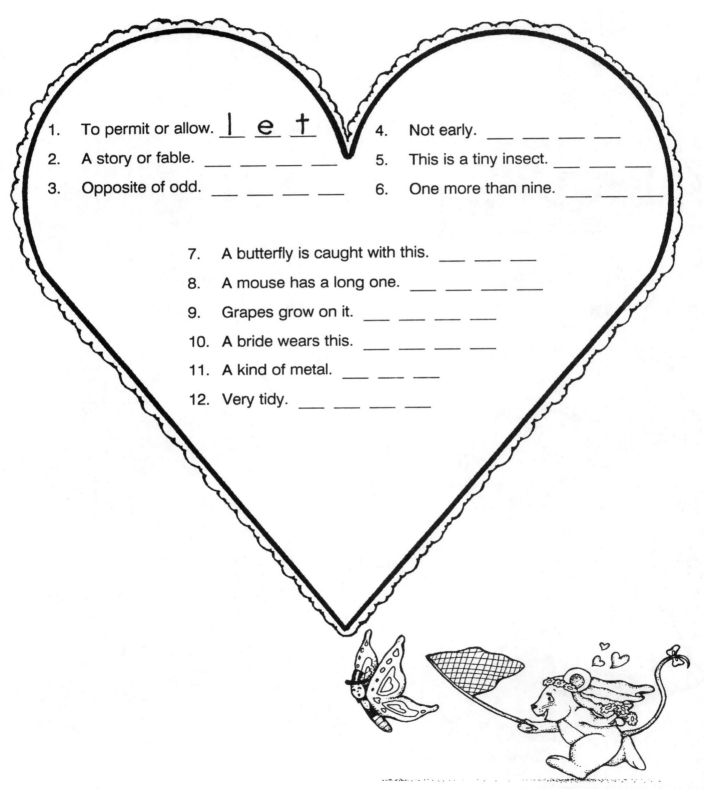

1. To permit or allow. l e t

2. A story or fable. ___ ___ ___ ___

3. Opposite of odd. ___ ___ ___ ___

4. Not early. ___ ___ ___ ___

5. This is a tiny insect. ___ ___ ___

6. One more than nine. ___ ___ ___

7. A butterfly is caught with this. ___ ___ ___

8. A mouse has a long one. ___ ___ ___ ___

9. Grapes grow on it. ___ ___ ___ ___

10. A bride wears this. ___ ___ ___ ___

11. A kind of metal. ___ ___ ___

12. Very tidy. ___ ___ ___ ___

Name _____ **Date** _____

President's Day

Directions: Cut and paste the President onto the correct coin or bill.

1¢

$5 $5

25¢

$20 $20

$1 $1

5¢   10¢

$10 $10

50¢

✂ -

February Bingo Gameboard

Directions: Copy the gameboard for each student. Hand out candy hearts for tokens. Use to reinforce spelling, math, science, or social studies skills.

Game Page

Scribbles—An Indoor Game

Materials Needed: crayons, black felt pen, paper

Make teams of two people. Provide each team
with a piece of paper. Allow each team member
to draw a "scribble" on the other's paper. Then,
using the crayons, direct the students to make a
picture out of this scribble. When all are finished,
share with the class and vote on the most creative,
funniest, etc. Display on a bulletin board entitled
"Scribble Salute."

Human Machines—An Outdoor Game

Here is another team game to be played outside. Divide the class into teams of 5 to 7
students each. Discuss how we use machines every day. Have students brainstorm
different types of machines (they can be small, such as a blender or large, such as a
train). Continue the discussion by explaining how there are usually quite a few moving
parts in a machine (like a clock). Then, have students in each team select a machine
and decide how they can "become" that machine. The other team(s) have to guess
what machine they are!

Poetry Page

Here are two poetry writing ideas that incorporate the sights, sounds, and smells all around us.

- **Triante (Triangle Poetry)**

Ground hog
Musky, Earthy
Fuzzy, Soft, Cuddly
Brown, Fearful, Fast, Shy
Digging, Burrowing, Hibernating, Looking, Chirping

Line 1: Title (1 word)   (Lines 2 through 5 refer to the title)

Line 2: Smells (2 words)

Line 3: Touch, Taste (3 words)

Line 4: Sight (4 words)

Line 5: Sounds/Actions (5 words)

- **Impressionistic Places Poems**

For a pre-writing activity, have students answer these questions about one of their favorite places; then have them re-write into poem form. See example.

1. What is the day like there? (1 or 2 words)

2. Favorite time of day there? (1 or 2 words)

3. What sounds do you hear there? (2 or 3 words)

4. What things do you see there? (2 or 3 things)

5. What do you most enjoy doing there? (2 or 3 things)

6. When will you go there again?

7. How will you feel then?

Disneyland

When its **warm** and **sunny**,
I like to be there at **noon**,
To hear the **band** and **people play**,
To watch **Mickey, Minnie,**
and **Pluto** dance,
While I **ride the Matterhorn**
and **big Carousel.**
I will be back again
this summer, and that
makes me smile inside!

Written by
Susan James

A Puzzling Message

Write your own Valentine message on the puzzle below. Then, cut out the pieces on the lines and place them in an envelope that you have addressed to that "special person." You can write a message to your best friend, or to a favorite relative, or to your teacher. Watch them have fun as they put the puzzle pieces together!

Cut on the dashed lines.

February Whole Language Unit:

HEROES ALL AROUND US

- How To Write A Unit
- Lessons
- Worksheets
- And More!

Hot Tips!

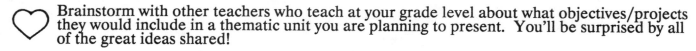

Brainstorm with other teachers who teach at your grade level about what objectives/projects they would include in a thematic unit you are planning to present. You'll be surprised by all of the great ideas shared!

Place a "Did You Know?" board in the hallway next to your door. Allow your students to write new knowledge or facts as they are learned. Other students and teachers will enjoy the new knowledge, too!

How To Plan

February is famous for its many heroes. George Washington, Abraham Lincoln, Charles Lindbergh, and Charles Dickens are just a few of the heroes born during this month. A hero is defined as someone who has great courage, nobility, and sacrifice, and is admired/honored for what he or she has accomplished. We can find heroes in real life and in literature. A woman who has contributed heroically to society is often referred to as a heroine.

This thematic unit has been designed to introduce a series of heroes and heroines to help students understand what a hero is and show them that they can be a hero to those around them.

1. Set the mood and introduce the unit by displaying the "Let's Build A Hero" bulletin board (directions on pages 69 to 75).

2. Assemble your resources: Books, films, tapes, games, texts, and real objects.

3. Plan general lessons integrating math, reading, art, music, language, and science.

4. Outline your lesson goals and objectives.

5. Make evaluation tools that are appropriate for the lesson.

6. After the first week of **hero** lessons, evaluate and then plan the next week.

Projects and Lessons

The following pages describe specific lessons and ideas that can be used to integrate the curriculum through the study of heroes.

- **Send home a newsletter** *(page 60) to inform parents of this month's activities, units, goals, and special activities. Have a student provide a poem or short story about heroes to include in the newsletter.*

Language

- **Make a Hero chart.** *As you are "building" the Hero Bulletin Board (pages 69 to 75), use the separate Hero Characteristics Chart (page 49) to allow students an opportunity to brainstorm synonyms for the words being discussed.*

Responsible	Brave	Honest	Solves Problems
cares obedient	daring confident unafraid	trustworthy	thinker wonder examine discover
Courageous	Thinker	Loyal	Risk-Taker
fearless	smart consider mediate figure out	dependable faithful sincere	adventurous bold

Math

- **Create a graph.** *Using various heroes and heroines have your students figure out how long each person lived...*

Louis Pasteur 1895
$$\begin{array}{r} 1895 \\ -1822 \\ \hline 73 \text{ years} \end{array}$$

Then create a comparison graph to show which heroes lived the longest, which lived the shortest, how many lived the same number of years, etc.

Social Studies

- **Divide the students into teams of 4 or 5.** *Be sure to include students of various strengths on each team. Announce that they are now going to be "Hero Hounds" and snoop around the school (and/or neighborhood) to find hometown heroes. Provide an information sheet (page 50) to gather their hero facts. Students will then rewrite their information in newsletter form and create a "Hometown Hero Herald" newspaper to share with friends, family, and/or fellow students!*

Projects and Lessons

Science

- **Re-create famous experiments.** *Experience this! After introducing a series of 4 or 5 famous scientific heroes, allow the students to do experiments similar to those done by the scientists. This can also be done for inventor heroes that have been presented.*

Creative Thinking Skills

- **Have an "Invention Connection" table displayed in the classroom.** *Make a poster display providing a pocket for the "Intend To Invent" (page 57) contracts and worksheet (page 39). Provide books and materials on various inventions. When students feel ready, have them fill out a contract form and begin their project. For a closure activity to the Hero Unit, have an Invention Connection Fair and allow students to present their inventions. Hand out certificates (page 58) to those who completed an invention project.*

Creative Writing, Social Studies, Public Awareness

- **Family Heroes Potluck** *Review the characteristics of what makes someone a hero. Lead students to the realization that those around us (including themselves) have some of these same qualities. Allow students to write a report on their mother, father, or family. Invite everyone to a family heroes potluck (page 56). After eating, have the students come forward with their hero(es) and present their report. It will be a hero-ific evening! (Use the clip art star medal on page 63 for name tags.)*

Projects and Lessons

Here is a handy list of people that you may wish to use in introducing your students to heroes. Information on these and other heroes and heroines can be found in encyclopedias, biographies, and other non-fiction works.

Patriotic Heroes

George Washington

Abraham Lincoln

Paul Revere

Sir John A. MacDonald

Thomas Jefferson

Betsy Ross

Explorers	Inventors/Scientists
Samuel De Champlain	Benjamin Franklin
James Cook	Alexander Graham Bell
Daniel Boone	Thomas Alva Edison
Matthew Henson	Louis Pasteur
Sacajawea	Walter Reed
Sally Ride	Marie Curie
John H. Glenn, Jr.	Albert Einstein
	George Washington Carver

Freedom Fighters	Authors/Musicians/Artisits
Harriet Tubman	Samuel Clemens (Mark Twain)
Sojourner Truth	Harriet Beecher Stowe
Susan B. Anthony	Louisa May Alcott
Dr. Martin Luther King, Jr.	Winslow Homer
Edgerton Ryerson	Thomas Chandler Haliburton
Dorothea Dix	Robert Frost
Elizabeth Cady Stanton	Gwendolyn Brooks
Frederick Douglass	Louis Armstrong

24

Name _____ **Date** _____

Hero Sandwiches

Work with a partner to "build" a hero sandwich to share!

Directions: Draw a line to match each ingredient with a characteristic. Match items that start with the same letter. The first one has been done for you.

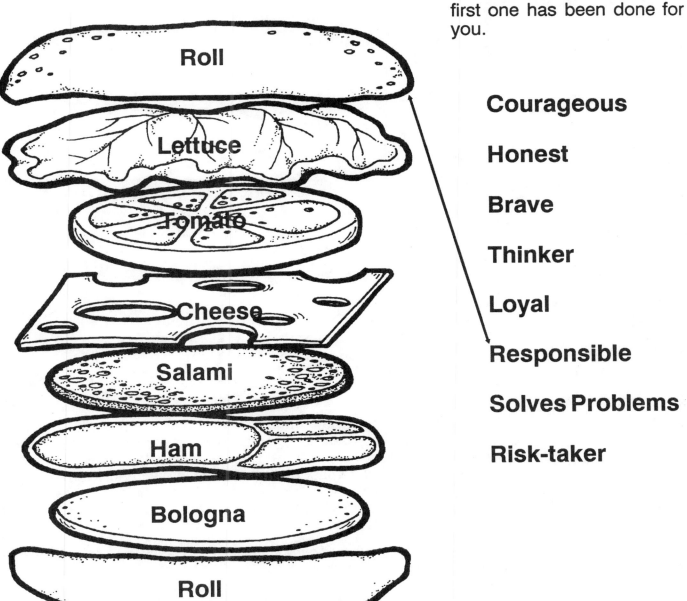

Roll

Lettuce

Tomato

Cheese

Salami

Ham

Bologna

Roll

Courageous

Honest

Brave

Thinker

Loyal

Responsible

Solves Problems

Risk-taker

♡ **Build your own hero sandwich:** Provide each "team" with one sandwich roll and a slice of the above ingredients. Have them build the sandwich by stating the hero characteristic as they add each layer. Then they can cut the sandwich in half and enjoy their hero building experience!

Math Facts Review

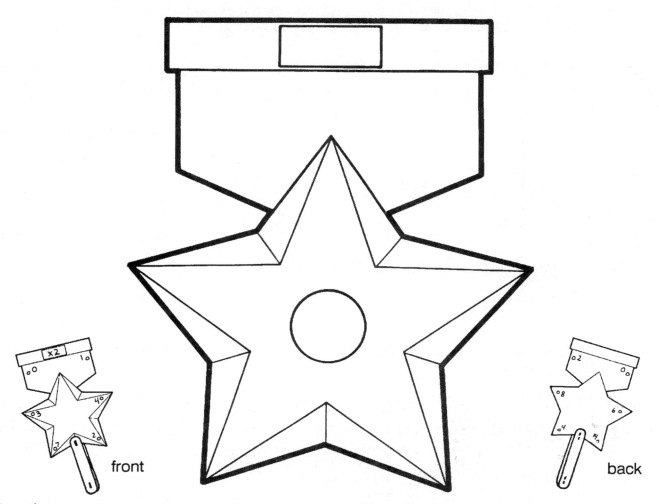

front

back

Directions: Make as many award shapes as you will need. Glue to heavy tagboard for durability; color and cut out. In the circle write an operation sign (see operation signs below) and the number you want to review (see diagram). Punch holes along the perimeter of the shape. Write a different number next to each hole punched. Turn the award over and write the answers to the problems next to the proper hole. Laminate and cut out. Staple two craft sticks together to the bottom of each award placing one stick on each side of the award (see diagram).

To Play: One child faces the front of the award, while another child faces the back of the award shape. The child facing the front puts a pencil through a hole next to a number and says the problem aloud. (In the diagram, for example, each number will be multiplied by two. If the child puts the pencil in the three, he would say, "T hree times two equals six." The child facing the back of the award shape checks the answers. After all problems have been computed, the children trade places.

Operation Signs: $+ , - , \times , \div$

Name _____ **Date** _____

Heroes Circle Graph

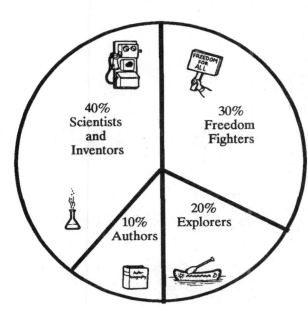

A graph gives us information quickly.

Use this pie graph to answer the questions below about these heroes:

Isaac Newton

Samuel Clemens

Susan B. Anthony

Samuel De Champlain

Albert Einstein

Frederick Douglass

Harriet Tubman

Ben Franklin

Christopher Columbus

Alexander Graham Bell

1. Divide the list of heroes into 4 groups: Freedom fighters, explorers, authors, and scientists/inventors.

2. Are more scientists/inventors or freedom fighters represented? _____

3. What two categories, when added together, will equal the same percentage as the freedom fighters (30%): _____(%) and _____(%)

4. Which heroes are represented the least? The most?

   Least _____

   Most _____

5. Make a bar graph showing the same information that is on the circle graph.

40%				
30%				
20%				
10%				
Heroes	Explorers	Science Inventors	Authors	Freedom Fighters

Fact or Opinion: How Do You Tell?

As we grow up we learn to tell the difference between what is true and what may or may not be true. It is called **fact** and **opinion**.

Fact – Something that is true and can be proven.

Opinion – A belief not based on something true. It is someone's feelings or ideas, and is based on what they think.

☆☆☆☆☆☆☆☆☆☆☆☆☆☆☆☆☆☆☆☆☆☆☆☆☆☆☆

Check the correct space.   **Fact**   **Opinion**

1. A person needs to breathe air to stay alive.   _____   _____

2. Apples taste sweet.   _____   _____

3. Trees are tall.   _____   _____

4. The day you were born is called your "birthday." _____   _____

5. Milk comes from cows.   _____   _____

6. The earth is round.   _____   _____

7. Short hair looks nice on girls.   _____   _____

8. A bird has feathers.   _____   _____

9. Riding a bicycle is fun.   _____   _____

10. Scary movies are fun to watch.   _____   _____

Open Worksheet

Directions _____

1.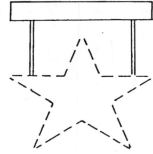

2.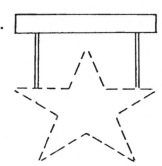

3.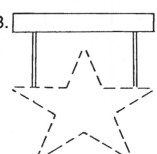

4.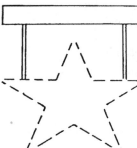

5.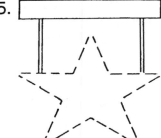

6.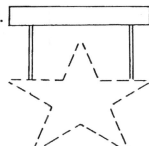

7.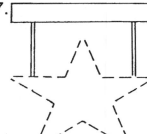

8.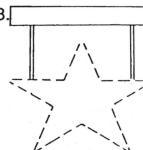

✂ — — — — — — — — — — — — — — — — — — —

Hero Quilt

A hero quilt is an excellent way for your students to display their knowledge of the heroes they are studying.

Materials Needed:

white paper, (cut into squares) crayons,

tape, stapler

Optional:

yarn, glitter, fabric, glue, string, clothespins

Directions:

1. Discuss/review concepts. Divide your class into teams of 3 or 4 students each.

2. Supply each team with materials and allow them to create the face of an appropriate hero.

3. When each team is finished, have them write the hero's name, along with their own (in small letters).

4. Tape the squares together, **taping them on the back side** to form the quilt.

5. Display on a bulletin board or wall space by stapling or use the optional method of hanging the Hero Quilt using a clothesline effect.

Special Note: The heroes can also be your students' family members; community workers; presidents or political leaders;local athletes; teachers; or any other special group you wish to focus on!

A Letter To My Hero

Draw a picture of your favorite hero. Then write a letter to tell why he or she is your favorite.

February People, Places, and Events

- ○ **Valentine's Day**
- ○ **George Washington**
- ○ **Abraham Lincoln**
- ○ **Dental Health Month**
- ○ **And More!**

Hot Tips!

♡ Take the Calendar of Events (pages 8 and 9) and make one copy for each student; attach to outside of an 11" x 17" piece of colored paper. As students learn the facts relating to each day's question, they can place worksheets or information notes inside the folder and use to review all of the new facts they have learned at the end of the month!

♡ Have your students make up their own worksheets in teams or pairs to help review the materials, skills, and concepts you have introduced.

Name _____ Date _____

Charles Lindbergh, Aviator
(Born February 4, 1902)

Charles Lindbergh was born on February 4, 1902. He lived on a farm. At a young age he showed an interest in machines, especially the airplane. In his later teen years he became a "barn stormer," a pilot who performed daredevil stunts at a fair or airshow.

After serving in the Army Reserves, he was hired to fly mail between St. Louis and Chicago. In 1927, he made his famous non-stop flight from New York City to Paris in 33 1/2 hours. He flew more than 3,600 miles (5,790 kilometers) without any stops! Lindbergh later invented cruise control for planes.

Hats off to Mr. Lindbergh!

1. **Knowledge**

   Name the historic flight Mr. Lindbergh made. Where did it begin? End? How long did it take?

2. **Comprehension**

   Create a class play re-telling the famous flight of the "Spirit of St. Louis."

3. **Application**

   Write a one page report stating why Mr. Lindbergh's invention of cruise control is helpful to aviators today.

4. **Analysis**

   Review the characteristics of a "hero." List the characteristics that Mr. Lindbergh appeared to have had, and explain why or how he showed these qualities.

5. **Synthesis**

   Charles Lindbergh's wife, Anne Morrow Lindbergh, was a writer and poet. Write a poem about her husband's flight from New York to Paris.

6. **Evaluation**

   Allow students to review informative materials on aircraft and flight. Discuss or list ways in which aircraft/flight have become an essential part of our daily lives.

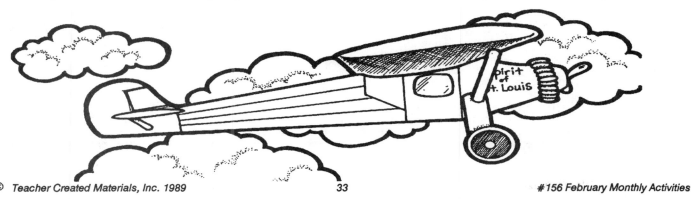

Heartful Expressions

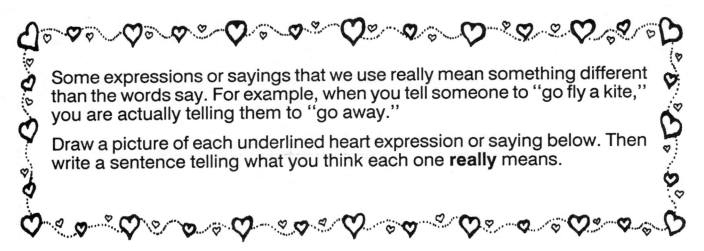

Some expressions or sayings that we use really mean something different than the words say. For example, when you tell someone to "go fly a kite," you are actually telling them to "go away."

Draw a picture of each underlined heart expression or saying below. Then write a sentence telling what you think each one **really** means.

He was <u>broken-hearted</u> when his dog died. _____ _____ _____	She has a <u>heart of gold.</u> _____ _____ _____
He wears his <u>heart on his sleeve.</u> _____ _____ _____	I don't <u>have the heart</u> to tell her. _____ _____ _____

Name _____   Date _____

George Washington Crossword

(Born February 22, 1732)

Directions: Read the clues. Fill in the boxes. Use the Word Bank.

Across

1) George learned to draw pictures of the land: A _ _ _.

4) He was the _ _ _ _ _ _ of our country.

5) He chopped down a _ _ _ _ _ _ tree.

6) Washington grew wheat and _ _ _ _ _ trees on his farm.

8) Mr. Washington fought for America's _ _ _ _ _ _ _.

Down

1) A subject George liked in school, _ _ _ _.

2) He was the first _ _ _ _ _ _ _ _ _.

3) Mr. Washington's first name: _ _ _ _ _ _.

4) George's birthday month: _ _ _ _ _ _ _ _.

7) Flag colors: _ _ _, white, and blue.

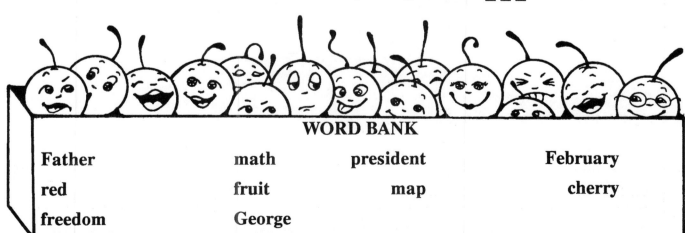

WORD BANK

Father	math	president	February
red	fruit	map	cherry
freedom	George		

Name _____   Date _____

Abe Lincoln's Groceries

(Born February 12, 1809)

When Abraham Lincoln was a young man, he worked in a store in New Salem, Illinois. Use the prices in the box below to figure out how much he would have sold these groceries for. One has been done for you.

 10 cents   16 cents   31 cents

13 cents   23 cents   50 cents

Example:

 10 cents

 + **31** cents
_____
41 cents

1.
 + _____

2.
 + _____

3.

 + _____

4.

 + _____

5.

 + _____

6.

 + _____

Challenge: How much would...

☆ 3 chickens cost? _____

☆☆ 5 sacks of flour cost? _____

☆☆☆ a "fish sandwich" cost? _____

Maple Leaf Word Changes

(Canada's Maple Leaf flag adopted February 15, 1965)

Directions: Make a new word by changing only one letter per line. Each letter change will make a new word, including the last change.

EXAMPLE:

DOG
DOT small mark
NOT can't do
NOD shake head

1.

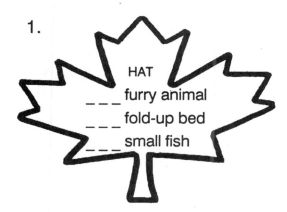

HAT
_ _ _ furry animal
_ _ _ fold-up bed
_ _ _ small fish

2.

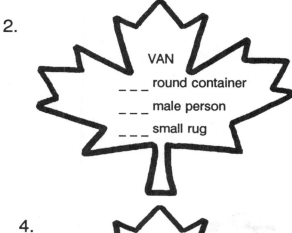

VAN
_ _ _ round container
_ _ _ male person
_ _ _ small rug

3.

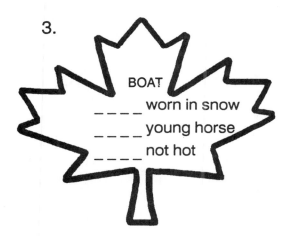

BOAT
_ _ _ _ worn in snow
_ _ _ _ young horse
_ _ _ _ not hot

4.

SLOW
_ _ _ _ wind does this
_ _ _ _ having blown
_ _ _ _ finished flight

5.

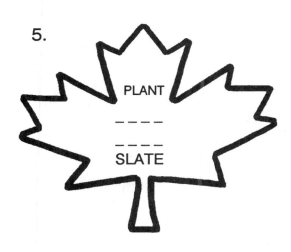

PLANT
_ _ _ _
_ _ _ _
SLATE

6.

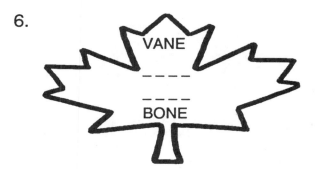

VANE
_ _ _ _
_ _ _ _
BONE

Name _____ Date _____

Teeth-erific Teeth

(February is Dental Health Month)

Animals have teeth, too! After looking up these animals in an encyclopedia or animal fact book, write the correct number of teeth each animal has.(You may want to use the **Tooth Bank**.)

horse

_____

pig

_____

lion

_____

wolf

_____

elephant

_____

dog

_____

beaver

_____

sheep

_____

cat

_____

cow

_____

camel

_____

rabbit

_____

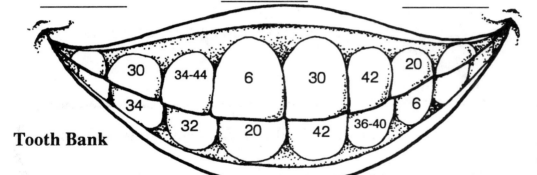

Tooth Bank

30   34-44   6   30   42   20
34   6
32   20   42   36-40

Challenge:

Make a list on the back of this page showing which animals have the same number of teeth.

A Healthy Smile
(February is Dental Health Month)

In the box below you will find pictures of some items that help you keep your teeth healthy and some other items that are not-so-healthy for your teeth. Write the word names of the items in the proper section of the chart.

These things help keep my teeth healthy.	These things are not-so-healthy for my teeth.
_____	_____
_____	_____
_____	_____
_____	_____

Use the Word Bank to help you spell words correctly.

WORD BANK

milk
fruits   toothpaste   candy   toothbrush   floss   bubble gum   soda pop

Invention Connection

(National Inventor's Day - February 11)

Match the inventor with the correct invention.

INVENTOR   **INVENTION**

Alexander Graham Bell

Cornelius van Drebbel

Leonardo da Vinci

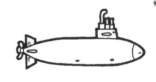

Ts'ai Lun

John Walker

Joseph F. Glidden

Galileo

Thomas Edison

Zacharias Janssen

☆For Fun: Look up these inventors and learn about their lives!

Alphabetical Order Hearts

(Valentine's Day - February 14)

Put the hearts on the arrow trail in alphabetical order.

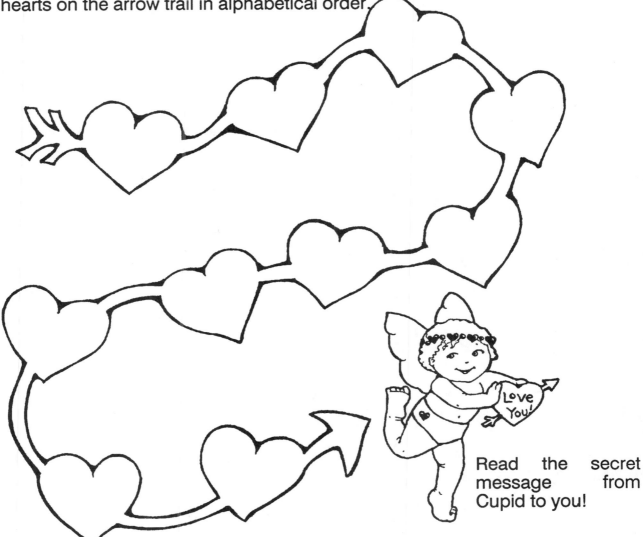

Read the secret message from Cupid to you!

✂ —

 people

 other

 friendly,

 so

 kind.

 Love

 Be

 they

 good,

 will...

Look Alikes

1. Find the four hearts that look exactly the same.

2. Color them exactly the same.

3. Color the other hearts different colors.

International Friendship Day

(February 19th)

Have a special Friendship Festival! Display pictures of friends, activities friends can do together, and so on. Use this pattern to make a chain of "friends" (self-portraits of students) that can be linked in a long line in the classroom, down the hall, and to where your Friendship Festival will be held. Include your grade level or the whole student body!

Directions: Reproduce one pattern for each child. Have students draw or color their face, hair and clothing on their pattern.

Ground Hog Day Poem...and Puppet Show!

Use the puppet pattern on this page, along with the stage (following page) to allow your students the opportunity to "be a ground hog" who comes out of his hole! After participating in this activity, why not let your students brainstorm and come up with an original Ground Hog Day Play!

Directions for stage (page 45). Cut out along solid black lines. (Students may wish to color stage brown.) Cut out hole (dotted lines). Fold flaps down and under. Tape Sections A together and Sections B together. Now "play" away!

How to Play:

Attach a wood craft stick to back left side of ground hog puppet. Slide through **left** side of stage to make the ground hog come out of his hole.

Directions for Puppets:

Reproduce ground hog shapes onto light brown construction paper. Color eyes, nose, ears, etc.; cut out.

44

Poem on Stage

A   B

↑ Fold Down ↑

Ground
Hog
Day
February
2nd

Silly little thing,
Does your
shadow
bring,
Something
that
tells me
when we
will have
spring?

cut out

↓ Fold Under ↓   ↓ Fold Under ↓

A   B

Name _____ Date _____

Buffalo Bill's Rootin'-Tootin' words
(Born February 26, 1846)

A **root word** is the part of a word that can stand alone. A beginning or ending can be added to the root word. **Directions**: Write the correct beginning or ending (prefix or suffix) to each root word below. Some words will have more than one.

redo = re + do   doing = do + ing

BEGINNINGS
dis - un - pre-

1. _____may

2. _____dress

3. _____roll

4. _____snap

5. _____miss

6. _____heat

7. _____school

8. _____tie

9. _____lock

10. _____test

ENDINGS
-ing -er -est

1. read_____

2. low_____

3. sing_____

4. hear_____

5. fast_____

6. play_____

7. farm_____

8. short_____

February Management

- ○ **Clip Art**
- ○ **Contracts and Awards**
- ○ **Holiday Report Form**
- ○ **A Month of Writing**
- ○ **And More!**

Hot Tips!

Arrange for another teacher to be "on call" for you (one who knows your class rules and management system), in case you are absent and you have a substitute. Then, if the substitute has a question, there will be someone to go to for assistance.

Use the sociogram (page 62) on a monthly basis to keep track of your students' socialization behaviors for any necessary child studies or screenings.

Name _____   **Date** _____

A Month of Writing

Here is a handy list of daily writing starters that will help your students develop skills in figurative speech. After each student has completed the day's extension, have the student expand by writing why he/she may feel or look as the sentence states.

1.	I am as cold as...	15.	I feel as smooth as...
2.	I feel as slippery as...	16.	I am as pointy as...
3.	I am as small as...	17.	I look as tired as...
4.	I feel as hot as...	18.	I am as busy as..
5.	I look as short as...	19.	I feel as smart as..
6.	I am as quiet as...	20.	I am as warm as...
7.	I feel as happy as...	21.	I look as round as..
8.	I am as tiny as...	22.	I feel as loved as...
9.	I look as silly as...	23.	I am as thankful as...
10.	I feel as big as...	24.	I am as excited as...
11.	I look as tall as...	25.	I feel as funny as...
12.	I am as proud as...	26.	I am as black as...
13.	I look as scared as...	27.	I feel as hard as...
14.	I am as soft as...	28.	I look as shiny as...

Heroes Characteristics Chart

Responsible	Brave	Honest	Solves Problems
Courageous	Thinker	Loyal	Risk-Taker

Hero Hound Information Sheet

Reporter's Name: _____

Class: _____

Goal/Objective: _____

_____

_____

Hometown Hero (Name)	WhatHero Has Done	Hero Characteristics

Check It Out!

Do you have a collection of books that you allow your students to take home to read? Here are two handy forms you can use to keep track of the books students check out.

Check It Out!

Student:_____ Date Checked Out_____

Book Title:_____ Date Checked In_____

My Favorite Part:_____

_____

_____

Please fold and place inside of the book you have chosen.

Staple a booklet together to keep in the check-out area.

	Student	Book Title	Date Out	Date In

February Record Form

NAME																	

Hooray For Homework!

Write your assignments in the spaces below. Lightly color over each section when assignments have been completed.

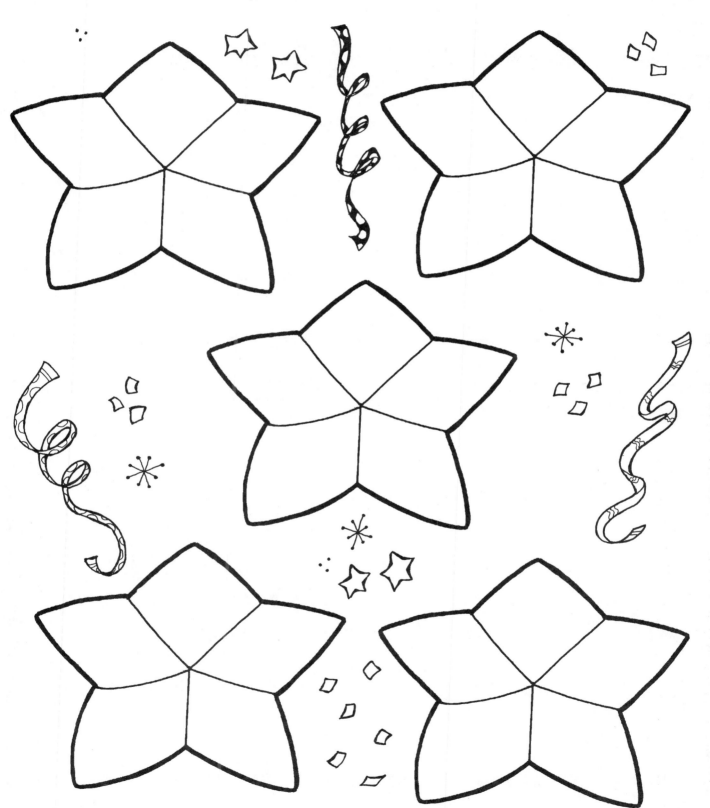

Invitation/Thank You

You're invited!

Thank you...

from the bottom of my heart.

54

Contract/Award

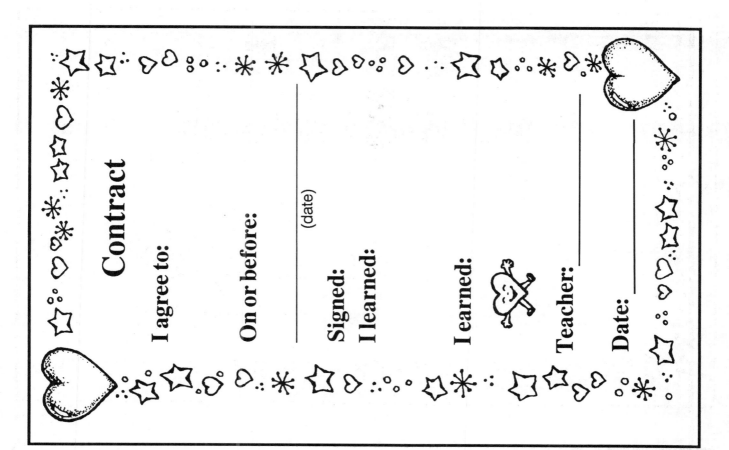

Contract

I agree to:

On or before:

_____
(date)

Signed:

I learned:

I earned:

Teacher:

Date:

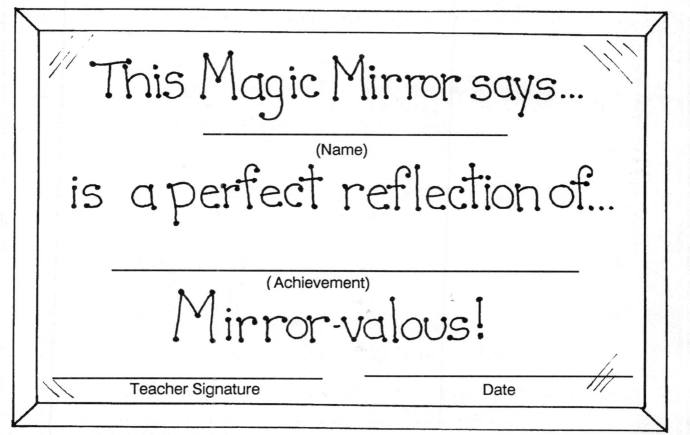

This Magic Mirror says...

_____
(Name)

is a perfect reflection of...

_____
(Achievement)

Mirror-valous!

_____
Teacher Signature

_____
Date

Potluck Supper Announcement

YOU!

Family Heroes Potluck

Please join us for a special night of friends food, and special family fun!

When:

Where:

Time:

Since it is a potluck, if your last name begins with:

A-G, please bring _____

H-Q, please bring _____

R-Z, please bring _____

✂ ☆☆☆☆☆☆☆☆☆☆☆☆☆☆☆☆☆☆☆☆☆☆☆☆☆☆☆

Please return this section!

Yes, we will be coming! _____

How many: _____

We will bring: _____

_____

Parent's Signature: _____

Child's Name: _____

Phone: _____

Invention Contract

I, _____

Intend To Invent

_____
(Idea or Title)

How it will work: _____

_____

_____

_____

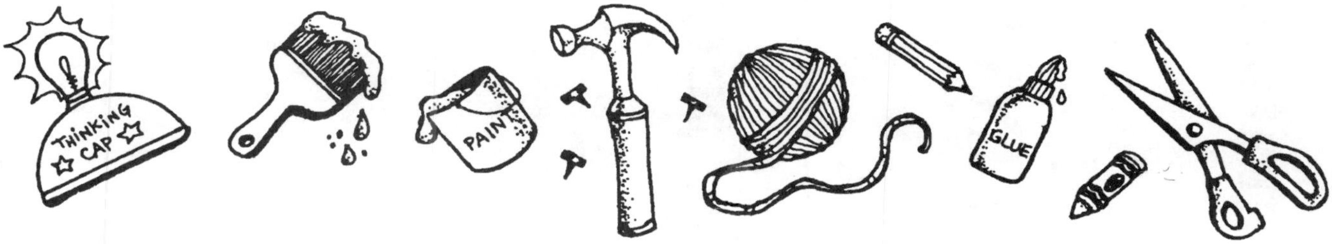

The supplies I will need: _____

_____

_____

_____

_____

_____

_____

_____

Teacher Approval: _____

Signed:_____ Date _____

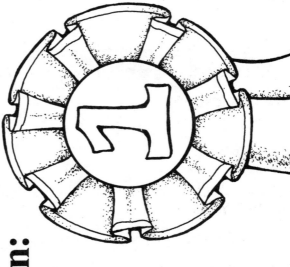

Congratulations!

_____ is a certified INVENTOR

Title of Invention: _____

First presented to the public on:

_____
(Date)

in

_____
(City and State)

_____
(Teacher)

_____
(Principal)

Love Bug Bookmark and Necklace

Here is a special gift your students can make for their Mom or Dad or other special person to show them their love!

Materials:

red yarn (32" long), red/white colored paper, small picture of student, scissors, glue, crayons

Directions for bookmark:

1. Cut out 2 red and 2 white hearts.

2. Glue picture of student onto 1 white heart. Write "I LOVE YOU" on the other white heart.

3. Color 2 red hearts to look like "love bugs."

4. Spread glue onto the back of 1 red and 1 white heart.

5. Sandwich one end of red yarn (cut into a 32" piece) between the two hearts.

6. Repeat with the 2 remaining hearts on the other end of the yarn. Let dry.

To make a necklace, follow the instructions above. Then, tie a small knot near "bugs" to form a necklace to be worn with love!

Pattern

Daily Schedule Board

Students often ask, "When will school be over today?" Here is a management system that will help students keep track of the day's events. It will also help them better understand the following concepts:

1. Time/Space Relationship
2. Before/After Relationship
3. Staying on Task
4. Responsibility

Directions:

1. Create a small bulletin board display as shown below.

2. Using sentence strips and a felt tip marker, write out all of the events that students will be engaged in that day: opening exercises, academic skills, specialists, special activities (class party, field trip), etc.

3. Each day before school, put the day's events (sentence strips) on the appropriate wall pocket space.

4. After each event has been completed, have an appointed student remove that strip and place it in a folder holder. At the end of the day, all the strips will be gone!

WALL POCKET CHART

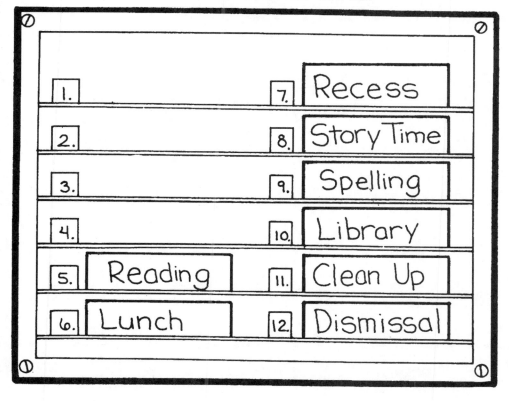

Folder Holder

Sociogram

Cooperative learning and student team teaching have become important educational tools. Here is a helpful way of observing friendship and learning patterns, as well as identifying students who do not interact, or who may be overbearing with others.

Directions: While students are engaged in free play or educational activities (centers, for example), observe how they interact. Record observations on the chart below. Make notes on the back of this sheet based on what you have written on the sociogram.

Circle = student

EXAMPLE: ———→ = student's preferred learning or play friend(s)

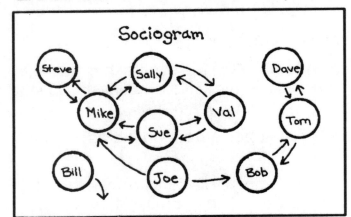

OBSERVATION CONCLUSIONS

■ Dave, Tom, and Bob stick together and don't allow others into their group.

■ The girls stick together, but appear to enjoy being with Mike, too.

■ Joe tries to interact, but is not really accepted into a group.

■ Bill is a loner, doesn't interact with classmates.

Sociogram

Clip Art

Valentine

1. Copy Valentine onto red or pink colored paper and cut out.

2. Cut slits on small Valentine and insert a small lollipop.

3. Have a special Valentine's Day party and give the Valentines to your class. Students always remember the "one from the teacher" the most!

64

Big Patterns

Big Patterns

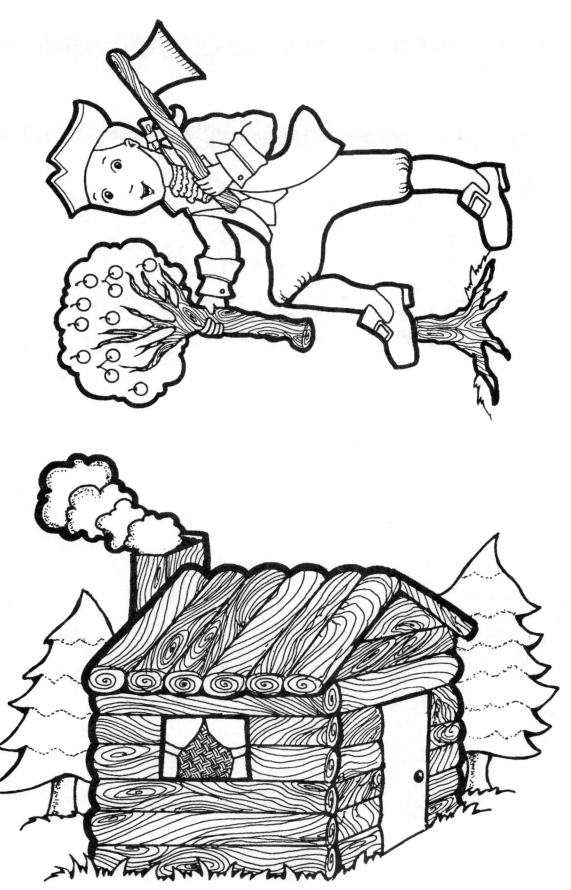

Big Patterns

Dear Parents,

February is a fun month, and we will be making many creative projects in the following weeks. Could you please help us by sending in any of the following items?

_____

_____

_____

_____

_____

_____

Thank you for your help!

_____

Teacher

Let's Build A Hero!

Responsible
Loyal
Thinker
Courageous
Solves Problems
Honest
Brave
Risk-Taker

Hidalgo
Tubman
King
Columbus
Washington
Curie

February
Bulletin Board

- Complete Directions
- Patterns
- Suggested Uses

Hot Tips!

Here's how to give bulletin board letters a 3-D effect: push a pin through the corners of each letter, then push the pins into the bulletin board. Gently pull the letters to top of the pinheads to create a space between the letter and the board.

Start a bulletin board photo file. Keep a camera handy to take pictures of completed bulletin boards. Keep in a file box for future reference!

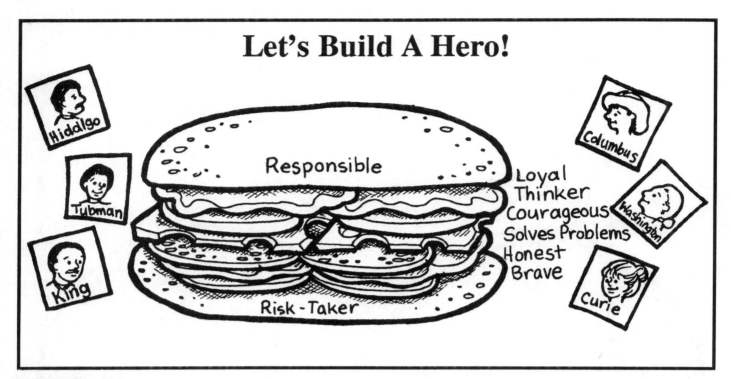

OBJECTIVE:

This interactive bulletin board has been designed to be "built" as part of an introductory lesson to "Heroes All Around Us." It can later be referred to as a review board and display area for hero - related activities.

MATERIALS

colored construction paper, stapler, scissors, pins, thick marking pen, fabric or butcher paper (for background)

CONSTRUCTION

- Reproduce patterns onto colored construction paper and cut out.
- Put up background and title.
- As the lesson is being taught, "build" the hero sandwich using class participation.

DIRECTIONS

- Have the students draw pictures of heroes as they learn about them (you may also include the heroes in their daily lives). Place the pictures around the sandwich.
- As a review, use red yarn to connect the picture of a hero with his or her characteristics .
- Use the "star badge" clip art (page 63) to write each of your students' names and a hero characteristic *they* have. Display around the sandwich.

Hot Tip!

♡ Old calendars make an excellent resource for pictures, photos, and cartoons to use for quick and easy bulletin board displays.

Let's Build A Hero (cont)

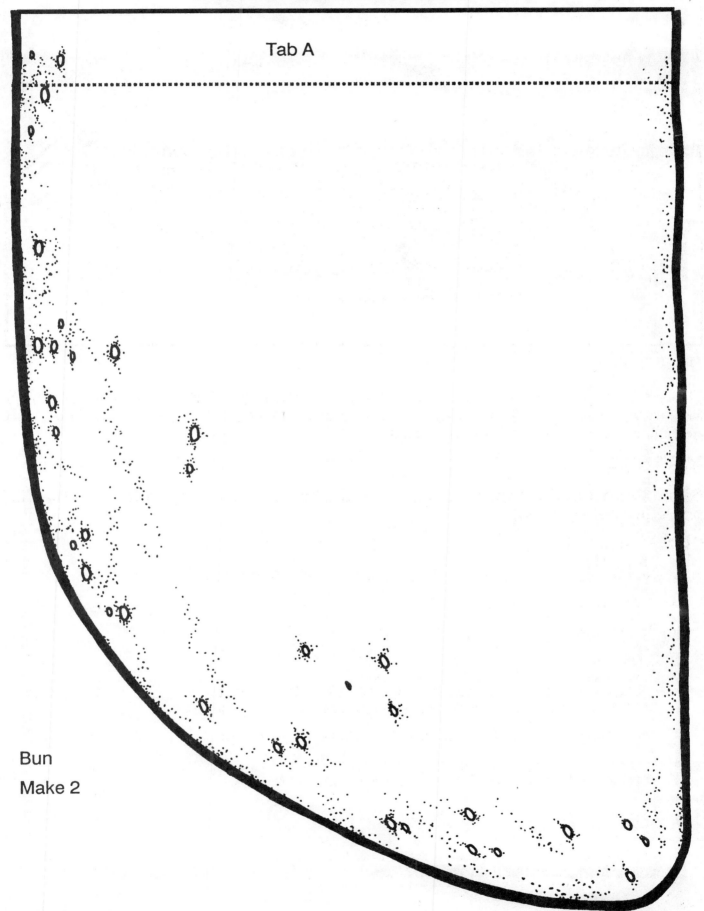

Tab A

Bun

Make 2

Let's Build A Hero!
(cont.)

Bun

Make 2

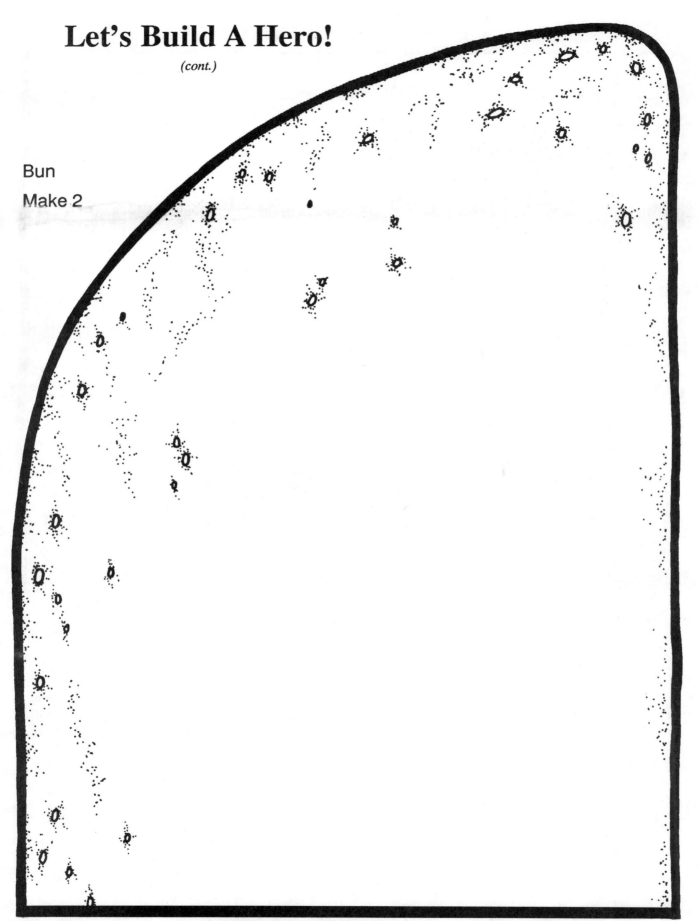

Attach on top of Tab A

Let's Build A Hero (cont.)

Lettuce
Make 3

Tomato
Make 3

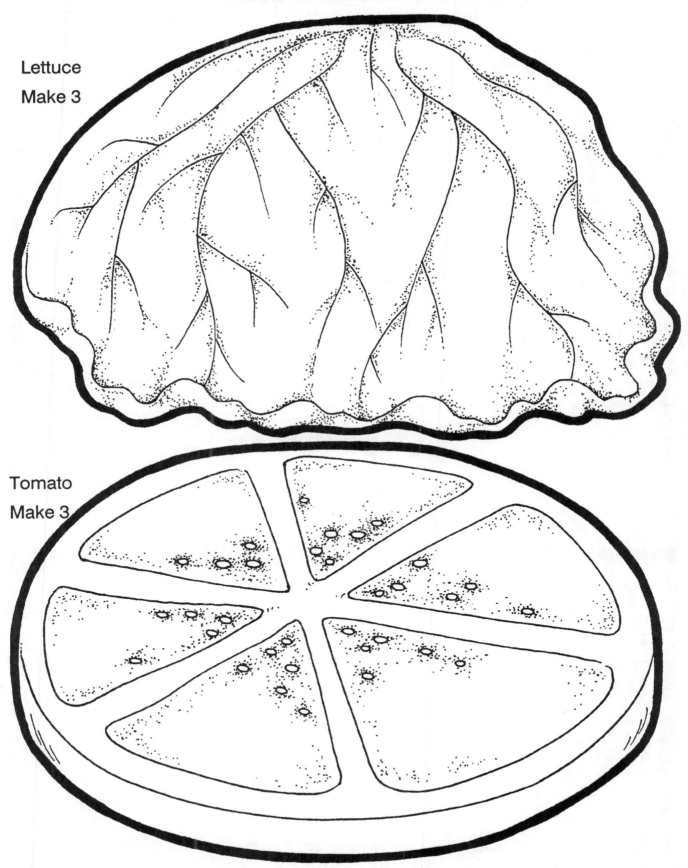

Let's Build A Hero! *(cont.)*

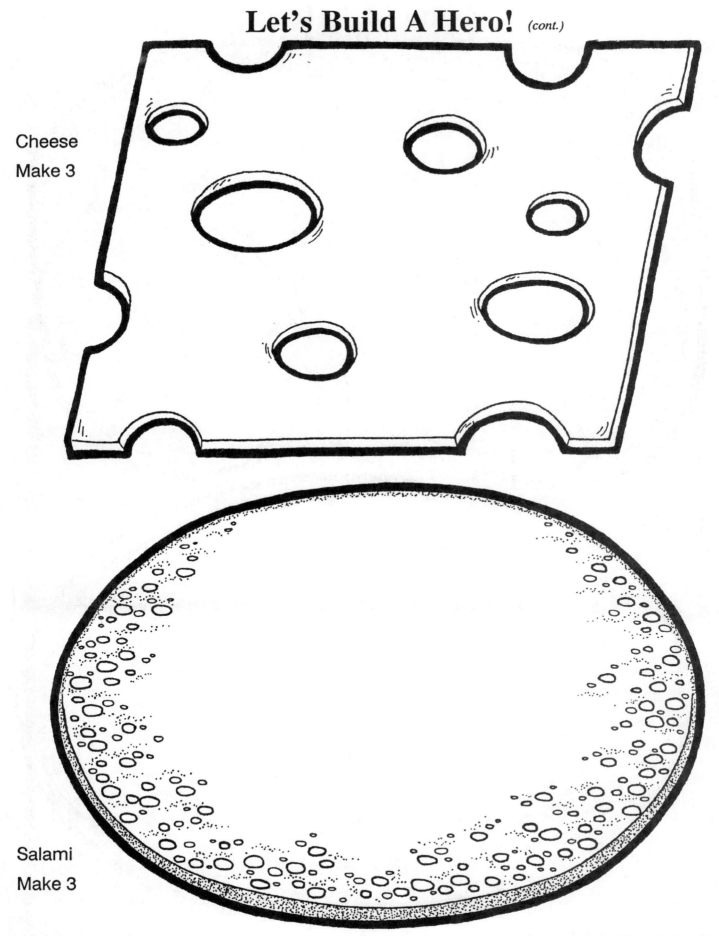

Cheese
Make 3

Salami
Make 3

Ham

Make 3

Bologna

Make 3

Answer Key

P. 8 & 9 Calendar of Events

1. Answers will vary.
2. Answers will vary.
3. A doctor
4. May 20 & 21, 1927
5. Answers will vary.
6. Westminster Abbey, London, England
7. Someone who writes.
8. Be prepared
9. Austria, Italy, France, Germany
10. 324
11. Answers will vary.
12. Near present-day Hodgenville, Kentucky
13. Boston, Massachusetts
14. The Roman god of love
15. 1965
16. A person who makes their own voice seem like it is coming out of another's mouth (usually a doll).
17. An animal that is so rare it may become extinct.
18. Nine
19. Answers will vary.
20. A person who offers a service for no charge.
21. 32 teeth
22. 1789
23. Answers will vary according to this year.
24. Northern Europe, near the Baltic Sea
25. A snow sled pulled by a team of 6 to 8 dogs.
26. William Frederick Cody
27. 18 miles; 29 kilometers
28. 301 days (302 in a leap year)
29. Every four years

P. 14

1. let
2. tale
3. even
4. late
5. ant
6. ten
7. net
8. tail
9. vine
10. veil
11. tin
12. neat

P. 15

1 cent - Abraham Lincoln
5 cents - Thomas Jefferson
10 cents - Franklin D. Roosevelt
25 cents - George Washington
50 cents - John F. Kennedy
$1 - George Washington
$5 - Abraham Lincoln
$10 - Alexander Hamilton
$20 - Andrew Jackson

P. 35

Across

1. map
4. father
5. cherry
6. fruit
8. freedom

Down

1. math
2. president
3. George
4. February
7. red

P. 36

1. 39 cents
2. 63 cents
3. 67 cents
4. 83 cents
5. 39 cents
6. 91 cents

150 cents or $1.50
50 cents

13 cents + 16 cents = 29 cents

P. 37

1. HAT
   CAT
   COT
   COD
2. VAN
   CAN
   MAN
   MAT
3. BOAT
   COAT
   COLT
   COLD
4. SLOW
   BLOW
   BLEW
   FLEW
5. PLANT
   PLANE
   PLATE
   SLATE
6. VANE
   CANE
   CONE
   BONE

Answer Key

P. 38

Horse - 36-40
Pig - 34-44
Lion - 30
Wolf - 42
Elephant - 6
Dog - 42
Beaver - 20
Sheep - 20
Cat - 30
Cow - 32
Camel - 34
Rabbit - 6

P. 40

Alexander Graham Bell - Telephone
Cornelius van Drebbel - Submarine
Leonardo da Vinci - Helicopter
Ts'ai Lun - Paper
John Walker - Matches
Joseph F. Glidden - Barbed Wire
Galileo - Telescope
Thomas Edison - Telephone
Zacharias Janssen - Microscope

P. 41

Be friendly, good, kind. Love other people so they will...love you.

P. 46

Beginnings:	Endings:
1. dis-	1. -er/-ing
2. un-	2. -er/-est
3. un-	3. -er/-ing
4. un-	4. -ing
5. dis-	5. -er/-est
6. pre-	6. -er/-ing
7. pre-	7. -er/-ing
8. un-	8. -er/-est
9. un-	
10. pre-	

Open Worksheets Skills

These pages are ready to use. Simply fill in the directions and write the skill you want to reinforce. Make a copy for each student or pair of students or glue the worksheet to tagboard and laminate. Place at an appropriate classroom center; students can use water-based pens for easy wipe off and subsequent use. Ideas and resources for programming these worksheets are provided below and on the following pages.

Math

Basic facts
Comparing numbers and fractions
Decimals
Word problems
Time
Place value
Skip counting
Ordinal numbers (1st, 2nd, 3rd, etc.)

Sets
Missing addends
Money problems
Geometric shapes
Measurement
Word names for numbers
Sequence
Percent

Roman Numerals

I - 1
II - 2
III - 3
IV - 4
V - 5

VI - 6
VII - 7
VIII - 8
IX - 9
X - 10

L - 50
C - 100
D - 500
M - 1,000
L - 50,000

Metric Measurement

mm - millimeter (1/10 cm)
cm - centimeter (100 mm)
dm - decimeter (100 cm)
m - meter (1,000 mm)
km - kilometer (1,000 m)

g - gram
kg - kilogram (1,000 g)
l - liter (1,000 ml)
ml - milliliter
cc - cubic centimeter

Measurement Equivalents

12 in. = 1 ft.
3 ft. = 1 yd.
5,280 ft. = 1 mi.

4 qt. = 1 gal.
2 pt. = 1 qt.
8 oz. = 1 c.

1 t. = 2,000 lbs.
60 sec. = 1 min.
60 min. = 1 hr.

Open Worksheet Skills

(cont.)

Abbreviations

Names of states	dr. - drive	mt. - mountain
Days of the week	ave. - avenue	p. - page
Units of measurement	Dr. - Doctor	etc. - et cetera
Months of the year	Mrs. - Misses	yr. - year
blvd. - boulevard	Mr. - Mister	wk. - week
rd. - road	Gov. - Governor	
st. - street	Pres. - President	

Contractions

isn't - is not	I've - I have	they'd - they would
doesn't - does not	we've - we have	you'll - you will
haven't - have not	I'm - I am	won't - will not
hasn't - has not	you're - you are	I'm - I am
that's - that is	it's - it is	let's - let us

Compound Words

airplane	bodyguard	everywhere	percent
anyhow	bookcase	footnote	quarterback
anything	cardboard	grandfather	snowflake
basketball	classroom	handwriting	suitcase
bedroom	earthquake	makeup	watermelon

Prefixes

dis -	**un -**	**over -**	**re -**
disapprove	uncut	overcharge	recover
discolor	uneven	overdressed	redo
discount	unfair	overdue	reheat
dislike	unhappy	overfeed	remiss
dismay	unlike	overgrown	replay
dismiss	unmade	overpaid	reset
disobey	unwashed	overrun	review

Suffixes

- ful	**- less**	**- ly**	**- en**
beautiful	ageless	actively	harden
careful	homeless	happily	moisten
helpful	priceless	quickly	sweeten
skillful	worthless	silently	thicken

Open Worksheet Skills

(cont.)

Plurals

- s

toe	kitten
pin	window
lamp	star
book	key

- es

church	class
lunch	inch
box	tomato
brush	waltz

- ies

sky	cherry
baby	body
party	army
family	lady

Anagrams

dear - dare - read
notes - stone - tones
fowl - flow - wolf
veil - vile - evil - live
tea - ate - eat

shoe - hoes - hose
vase - save
pea - ape
north - thorn
flea - leaf

veto - vote
cone - once
stop - tops - pots - post - spot
steam - meats - mates - tames

Synonyms

sleepy - tired
firm - solid
story - tale
shut - close
easy - simple

wealthy - rich
quick - fast
sea - ocean
icy - cold
chore - task

friend - pal
tiny - small
jump - leap
gift - present
hike - walk

Antonyms

empty - full
tame - wild
city - country
faster - slower
strong - weak

tall - short
rough - smooth
light - dark
dirty - clean
calm - nervous

correct - wrong
forget - remember
thick - slender
sweet - sour
young - aged

Homonyms

eight - ate
whole - hole
red - read
hour - our
peace - piece
lone - loan

pale - pail
knew - new
nose - knows
blew - blue
would - wood
for - four - fore

by - buy - bye
sense - cents - scents
two - too - to